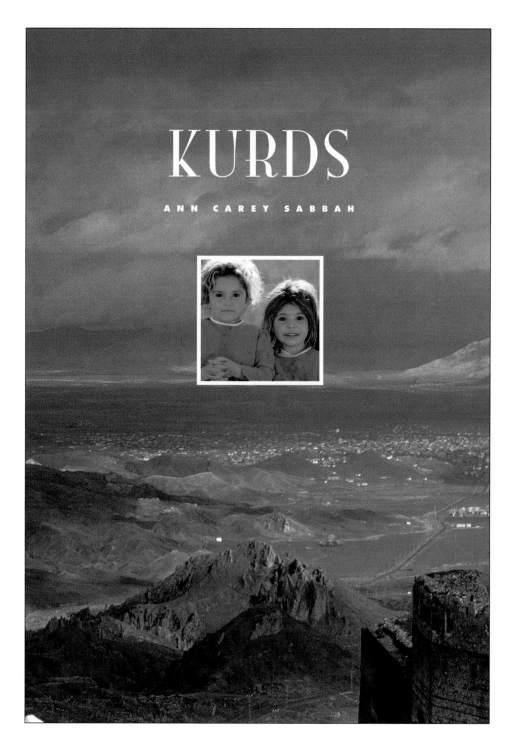

KURDS

ANN CAREY SABBAH

SMART APPLE MEDIA MANKATO MINNESOTA

Published by Smart Apple Media
123 South Broad Street, Mankato, Minnesota 56001

Produced by The Creative Spark, San Juan Capistrano, CA
    Editor: Elizabeth Sirimarco
    Designer: Mary Francis-DeMarois
    Art Direction: Robert Court
    Page Layout: Jo Maurine Wheeler

Photos/Illustrations: A. Woolfit/WoodfinCamp/PNI 4, 6; Lee Day/Black
Star/PNI 7; Max Engel/Woodfin Camp/PNI 8-9, 22, 27; Kevin Davidson
10; Hulton-Deutsch Collection/Corbis 12; Barry Iverson/Woodfin
Camp & Associates/PNI 13, 16; Frank Fournier/Contact Press
Images/PNI 14; Charles Crowell/Black Star/PNI 15, 19, 23, 26;
Bruno Barbery/Magnum/PNI 20; Ann Purcell; Carl Purcell/Words
& Pictures/PNI 24

Library of Congress Cataloging-in-Publication Data
Sabbah, Ann Carey 1965–
    Kurds / by Ann Carey Sabbah.
       p. cm. — (Endangered cultures)
    Includes bibliographical references and index.
    Summary: Traces the history of the Kurdish people, who live mainly
in the mountainous region where the borders of Iraq, Iran, and Turkey
converge, and discusses their struggles to preserve their culture and
establish their own country of Kurdistan.
    ISBN 1-887068-92-9 (alk. paper)
    1. Kurds—Juvenile literature. 2. Kurdistan—Juvenile literature.
[1. Kurds.] I. Title. II. Series.
DS59.K86S3 1999
909'.0491597—dc21   98-36150

First edition

9 8 7 6 5 4 3 2 1

Table of Contents

Who Are the Kurds? 5

History of the Kurdish People 11

Strangers in Their Own Land 17

Loss of a Culture 25

Glossary 29

Further Reading and Information 31

Index 32

*The Kurds are the largest ethnic group in the world without
a country of their own.*

Who Are the Kurds?

The Kurds are a group of people who live mainly in a mountainous region of the **Middle East**. This region was once known as Kurdistan. In the first part of the 20th century, a treaty divided Kurdistan, and although the Kurds wanted a country of their own, they became residents of Iraq, Iran, Syria, and Turkey.

As of 1998, an estimated 22 million Kurds live in the countries that make up the region formerly known as Kurdistan. They have a typical style of dress and many unusual traditions that set them apart from the other residents of the countries where they live. Because they are different, Kurds suffer **persecution,** and some have moved to other places in Europe and the Middle East. About 400,000 Kurds live in Germany, for example.

Kurds have always been farmers and shepherds. For thousands of years, they lived as **nomads,** moving about to find good pasture land or fertile soil. Even today, many Kurds raise goats, sheep, or cattle in pastures high in the mountains. Their herds provide milk, meat, and cheese

1174

A Kurdish warrior named Saladin becomes the king of Egypt and Syria.

For many hundreds of years, Kurds have raised livestock, often living as nomads to find the best places to graze their animals.

for their families. They also supply wool and leather to be sold in the market. Kurdish farmers grow fruits, vegetables, and wheat. In fact, they grow up to one-third of the grain that is produced in the region. The Kurds also grow crops such as cotton and tobacco.

Some Kurds are still nomads, changing pastures with the seasons. Shepherds set up permanent tents made of heavy, black wool in the winter pastures. When traveling higher into the mountains during warmer seasons, nomadic Kurds use tents made from lighter fabrics that are easy to carry and set up. Camps usually consist of many families that herd their flocks together.

Some Kurds live in bigger towns of up to a few thousand people on the lower slopes of the mountains. These people usually work as shopkeepers, tradesman, artisans, or teachers. In villages and towns, Kurds live in permanent homes of clay and stone built up the sides of a hill. An **extended family** shares a Kurdish home.

About 75 percent of Kurds are Sunni Muslims, a group of people who follow the religion of **Islam.** They believe in Allah (the Islamic word for God) and the revelations of a prophet known as Muhammad. The religious leader of a Kurdish community, called a *sheikh,* is usually involved when something important happens in the community, such as a wedding or a funeral.

1639

The Ottoman and Persian Empires sign the treaty of Qasr-i-Shirin, making their frontier in the Kurdish mountains.

A bearded Kurdish vendor bargains with his customer at a Turkish fruit market. These men live in Erzurum, a city in eastern Turkey where Kurds make up the majority of the population.

Colorful Clothing

The bright colors and unusual beauty of traditional Kurdish attire stand out among other clothing styles in nations where they live.

Women wear two dresses, one on top of the other. Intricate embroidery decorates the dress worn on the outside, called a *gambaz*. It has a low neckline to show off the fabric of the dress worn underneath.

Beneath the dresses are long, tight-fitting pants. Scarves are tied snugly at the women's hips, with colorful aprons tied over the scarves. Some women wear a type of turban on their heads, made from a scarf like that worn around the waist. A sheer veil on top of the turban often has sequins or beads sewn at the edges.

Traditional costume for Kurdish men includes an open-necked shirt, called a *sherwall,* with a vest worn over it. Pants are loose and baggy, with a wide sash at the waist. Kurdish men also wear turbans on their heads.

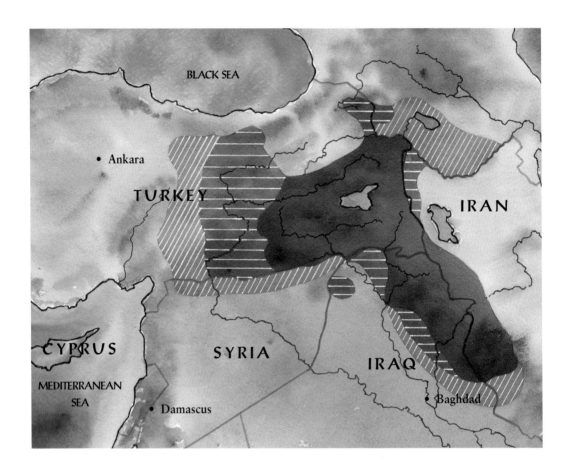

KURDISH DISTRIBUTION
across Iran, Iraq, Syria, & Turkey

 75-100%

 30-75%

 Under 30%

The majority of Kurds live in the mountainous regions where the borders of Iran, Iraq, Syria, and Turkey come together. In some parts of the region, the population is almost entirely Kurdish. Note the portion of the population in each area made up of Kurdish people.

History of the Kurdish People

The Kurds probably descended from Indo-European tribes that migrated to the Kurdistan region around 4,000 years ago. Scholars believe they descended from the Medes, a group of people who inhabited part of ancient Persia (now called Iran).

The Kurds followed Zoroastrianism, a religion founded in Persia during the sixth century B.C. The Zoroastrians worshiped a supreme god and believed in the importance of doing good to combat evil. Then, during the seventh century A.D., the Arabs became a strong force and brought the Islamic religion to the region. The people who lived in the area converted to Islam, but the Kurds did manage to maintain some political independence.

Powerful neighbors have always surrounded the Kurds—first the Persians, then the **Byzantine Empire,** and finally the **Ottoman Empire.** The Kurds relied on the difficult mountainous terrain where they lived to avoid being conquered by their neighbors.

During the **Crusades,** when Christians tried to bring their religion to countries around the world, Muslim Kurds and Arabs united to fight the Christian crusaders. One

Sheik Ubaidullah tries to convince the British consul to establish an official Kurdistan.

of the most famous and respected warriors was a Kurdish man named Saladin. He became the king of Egypt and Syria in 1174.

For nearly 600 years, the Ottoman Empire, which controlled the Islamic world, reigned over the Kurds. Ottoman rule lasted until the end of World War I in 1918. During negotiations after the war, Britain and France proposed the formation of an independent Kurdistan. They even signed the Treaty of Sèvres in 1920, which established a Kurdish state. But there were those who had different ideas, and Kurds in the region soon found themselves governed by Turkish laws.

Enemies of the Ottoman Empire imprisoned Arabs, Kurds, and Persians during World War I. When the empire fell at the end of the war, the Kurds were the only group denied a homeland.

*Many Kurds have lived in a constant state of war
since the end of World War I.*

*World War I ends.
Britain and France
propose the
formation of an
independent
Kurdish state.*

The Treaty of Lausanne, signed in 1923, officially divided Kurdistan. Most Kurds found themselves living in Turkey, although they eventually were divided into what became Iraq, Iran, Syria, and parts of the former Soviet Union. This division caused many problems for the Kurdish people. It also inspired them to struggle for independence from the governments of countries in which they lived.

*Other ethnic groups often persecute the Kurds in the countries where
they live, forcing them to seek refuge elsewhere.*

THE LEGEND OF ZAHHAK

Many Kurds feel a strong connection to the mountains because of a popular myth about the origins of their culture. This myth says the Kurdish people descended from children who hid high in the mountains to escape a child-eating giant named Zahhak.

According to Kurdish folklore, Zahhak was a terrifying giant with snakes growing out of his shoulders. The devil came to Zahhak and told him there was only one way to get rid of the snakes. He would have to feed them the brains of two children every day.

Zahhak decided to try this strange cure, and so he assigned an executioner to bring him the children's brains. The executioner took pity on his victims, and instead of hurting any children, he brought him the brains of sheep.

The children escaped to the safety of the mountains. They hid there and became a new group of people known as the Kurds. Legend says that one of the children finally killed Zahhak.

Today Kurds celebrate their New Year, called *Nowruz*, on March 21st, the anniversary of the death of Zahhak.

1920

The Treaty of Sèvres is signed, recognizing Kurdistan.

An Iraqi Kurdish woman prepares to fight. Kurds in Iraq
still hope to win their freedom one day, although the government
continues to oppose them.

Strangers in Their Own Land

The Kurds continue to have a difficult history in the Middle East. For example, although they make up almost one-quarter of the Iraqi population, they still suffer severe **discrimination** and mistreatment by the government.

The Kurds came close to gaining independence in Iraq 50 years after the Treaty of Lausanne was signed. From 1970 into the mid-1980s, Kurdish became one of the country's official languages. Kurdish school children could learn lessons in their native tongue. In 1974, the Kurds—with support from Iran—held serious discussions with the Iraqi government about plans to set up an independent Kurdish state.

Unfortunately, the Iraqis dashed Kurdish hopes one year later. Conservative Iraqi leaders feared signing any border agreement that would mean less land for their nation. Iran signed the Algiers Agreement, promising to end their support of the Kurds. Without Iran, the Kurds posed little threat to Iraq.

1923

The Treaty of Lausanne is signed, dividing Kurdistan.

Such poor treatment angered Iraqi Kurds. Some even decided to fight against their own country in the Iran–Iraq War (1980–1988). The government of Iraq did not want the Kurds to join their enemy's army, so they attacked several Kurdish villages with poisonous gas.

One such village was Halabja, a Kurdish town in the southern portion of Kurdish Iraq. Halabja is famous for its writers and poets, but Iraq viewed the 50,000 townspeople as troublemakers who had resisted the government for too long. On March 16, 1988, Iraq dropped deadly bombs that showered the town with poisonous chemicals. These chemical weapons immediately killed thousands of people, but the bombardment continued for three days.

By the end of the attack, 5,000 people—mostly women and children—were dead. Bodies filled the streets. Animals lay dead. Plants and trees withered as well. The assault wounded thousands of people, and years later, survivors struggle with grave ailments. Some are blind or have serious skin diseases. Babies are born dead or with birth defects. Cancer rates are abnormally high, especially among children.

Unfortunately, nations around the world virtually ignored what had happened. Some were even partially to blame. The United States and other western nations had supplied Iraq with the chemicals used to make the bombs, and Turkey helped deliver them to Iraqi government officials.

In 1991, following the Gulf War, the movement toward Kurdish independence regained momentum. Groups rose up against the government of Iraq in another attempt to form an independent Kurdish state.

This uprising angered the government of Iraq, and they punished the Kurdish rebels by dropping bombs on villages in the north. Many people died. At least one million Kurds fled over the mountains into neighboring Iran and Turkey. Some people were allowed to stay, while others were forced to live in refugee camps in the mountains. Life in the camps was very difficult. Temperatures were cold, and there wasn't enough food or shelter, so thousands starved or froze to death.

1946

Mustafa Barzani starts the Kurdish revolt against Iran.

When the Iraqi government attacked villages in 1991, one million Kurds fled in fear of what their own government might do to them next. They took refuge in the mountains of Turkey, carrying their possessions across rugged and dangerous terrain to set up camps. Both Turkish and Iraqi armies continued to harass them along the border of the two countries.

Talks between Kurds and the Iraqi government break down. Kurdish independence is not granted.

An artist draws a portrait of General Mustafa Barzani, a Kurdish nationalist who led his people in a 1946 revolt against Iran.

Estimates suggest that 100,000 Kurds have been killed in Iraq since the mid-1970s. The 3.8 million Kurds of Iraq still worry about possible attacks on their towns. Men and women carry guns and stand guard, watching for signs of danger. A Kurdish freedom fighter is called a *peshmerga*, which means "one who faces death." Many *peshmergas* still live in camps in the Zagros mountain range that forms the border between Iraq and Iran.

Kurds in Iran also fight for their independence. **Nationalist** Kurds have struggled with the government of Iran to form a country of their own.

Before the turn of the century, a Kurdish hero named Sheikh Ubaidullah launched a revolt against the ruler of Persia. With the help of British troops, another *sheikh*, Mahmoud Berezendji, struggled for control of Kurdish regions after World War I. He called himself the King of Kurdistan.

In 1946, at the end of World War II, a Kurdish nationalist named Mustafa Barzani led a widespread uprising in Iran. For a very short time, the Kurds established their own state, with the capital at Mehabad, a city in the Kurdish region of Iran. Iran's armed forces ultimately defeated the attempt at independence.

In the 1980s, the Iranian government briefly considered some measures that would allow the Kurds to gain some independence. The government, however, did not want its people to be divided. Their decision was based on the religious belief that all Muslims are of one faith— even if they speak different languages.

During the Iran–Iraq War, Iran allowed many Kurdish refugees to cross the border if the men would agree to fight with their army in the war against Iraq.

Difficulties between the Kurds and the Turkish government go back to 1923, when Turkey first became an independent state. The leader at that time, Mustafa Kemal Ataturk, became known as the Father of the Turks.

Turkey was a brand-new country, and Ataturk wanted to make everyone in the country a Turk. He refused to see the Kurds as a unique people and made strict laws that banned Kurdish language, dress, and tradition. The government insisted they were not Kurds, but "Mountain Turks."

The Kurds fought heroically in the years following the formation of the Turkish state, and thousands died in the process. Then, in the late 1960s, oil was discovered in the southeastern part of Turkey where a large portion of

1975

Iran and Iraq sign a border agreement. Iran no longer offers aid to Iraqi Kurds.

21

Mass arrests of Kurds occur following a Turkish military coup. The Iran–Iraq War begins.

A pair of Kurdish farm workers build a haystack in the mountains of Turkey. When oil was discovered on lands occupied by the Kurds, the Turkish government exerted even greater control over the Kurdish population, attempting to prevent a rebellion.

the Kurdish population lived. The government became even more interested in maintaining control over the Kurds. They did not want revolts to interfere with the money that could be made from oil production.

Regardless of the pressure to live as Turkish citizens, the Kurds in Turkey have not forgotten their heritage, and they continue to fight for independence. In the 1970s, a group of Kurdish rebels established a strong political party known as the PKK, or the Kurdistan Workers Party. One faction of the PKK is a fierce military group, which has fought against both the Turkish army and the police.

The PKK grew from a movement started by a group of intellectuals who wanted the government of Turkey to officially recognize the Kurdish language. They believed all people should be treated equally, regardless of their race or social class.

The PKK believes an independent Kurdish state should be established in Turkey. They envision a Kurdish state that will eventually include regions of Iraq, Iran, and Syria. Because of the PKK's reputation for violence, not all Kurds support it. Some also disagree with the communist ideals of the PKK, particularly the belief that agriculture should be controlled by the government. Nonetheless, the PKK continues to be a powerful force in the struggle for Kurdish independence.

1984

The first attacks by the PKK take place in Turkey.

Two young Kurdish fighters display their weapons, a rifle and an RPG-7 anti-tank rocket.

Kurdish women who live in Iran, like all female residents of that country, wear the Muslim head covering and veil known as a chador. *Traditional Kurdish clothing is not permitted by the Iranian government.*

Loss of a Culture

What does it mean to lose a culture? In the case of the Kurds, it means many things—including the loss of traditions and language. While the Kurds continue to struggle for independence, the governments of the countries where they live often try to suppress cultural differences. They hope that if everyone is more alike, no group will attempt to divide the country.

As other societies **assimilate** the Kurds, traditional Kurdish dress has begun to disappear. Kurdish women in Iran must wear an Iranian head covering, called a *chador*, instead of their own traditional clothing. Some Kurds feel that Kurdish dress sets them apart from other citizens and may cause people to discriminate against them. Today Kurds often seem just like anyone else in the countries where they live.

The younger generation in particular has stopped wearing traditional clothing, preferring Western styles, such as jeans. They often stop speaking Kurdish, too. Teachers discourage Kurdish children from speaking their language at school and teach in the native language of the country where they live—Turkish in Turkey, Arabic

1988

The Iraqi army commits a deadly massacre at Halabja, killing at least 5,000 Kurds.

in Iraq and Syria, and Persian in Iran. It is much more difficult for students to do well at school when they have to learn a new language in addition to learning their lessons.

Outside of their homes, Kurdish children rarely hear their native language spoken. They hear Turkish, Arabic, or Persian on the television and radio. Fewer and fewer people know how to speak Kurdish, so the language is gradually disappearing.

As of 1998, approximately 26 million Kurds live around the world without a country of their own, discouraged from practicing their traditional way of life.

While some Kurdish men and women still dress in traditional clothing, young people prefer the casual styles that are popular around the world.

A Kurdish parliament is elected in northern Iraq.

Finally, competition for natural resources poses a threat to Kurdish culture. The governments of Iraq, Iran, and Turkey rely on natural resources to build their economies. Kurdish regions are rich in many key natural resources.

The mountainous regions where the Kurds live are an important source of water for both Iraq and Iran. Water is a valuable resource in these countries. Dams have been built to store water and to create **hydroelectric** power. The governments of Iraq and Iran do not want to lose control of the Kurdish regions because then they would also lose control of water resources.

The Kurds will not stop fighting for independence willingly. They understand that without a country of their own, they may lose their unique traditions, language, and way of life. Many Kurds believe that establishing their own country, which would be called Kurdistan, is the only way to save their culture. The countries that now occupy the region will not hand over the land. The Kurds have a saying: To be a Kurd means looking death in the eye. To be a Kurd, one must be courageous. One must be committed to Kurdistan. The struggle for a Kurdish homeland—and to save the Kurdish culture—will continue.

Glossary

assimilate   To absorb the traditions of a population or people within a community.

Byzantine Empire   The eastern half of the Roman Empire, in power from the 4th through the 11th centuries, whose ancient Christian capital, Byzantium, is now Istanbul, Turkey.

Crusades   Missions undertaken by Christian powers to win the Holy Land from Muslims in the 11th, 12th, and 13th centuries.

extended family   A family unit that is made up of not only parents and children, but grandparents, aunts, uncles, and cousins also.

discrimination   Punishment or poor treatment for being different.

hydroelectric   Related to the production of electricity using water power.

Islam   The religion of the Muslim people, including the belief of Allah as God and Muhammad as his prophet.

Middle East   The countries of Southwest Asia and Northern Africa, extending from Libya to the west to Afghanistan on the east.

nationalist   Someone who strongly supports the interests of and feels a sense of pride in his or her nation. Kurdish nationalists hope to one day have a nation of their own.

nomads	Individuals who travel from place to place and do not have a fixed home.
Ottoman Empire	The Arab empire that led the Islamic world for about 600 years, from 1299 to 1923. Constantinople (formerly Byzantium and now Istanbul, Turkey) became the capital of the empire in 1453.
persecution	The act of harassing or attacking individuals or groups, usually because they are of a different origin, religion, or race.
peshmerga	A Kurdish word for a freedom fighter.
sheikh	A religious leader of the Islamic religion.

Further Reading and Information

BOOKS:

Laird, Elizabeth. *Kiss the Dust*. New York, NY: Puffin Books, 1994.

O'Connor, Karen. *A Kurdish Family*. Minneapolis, MN: Lerner Publications, 1996.

Steins, Richard. *The Mideast After the Gulf War*. Brookfield, CT: Milbrook Press, 1992.

WEB SITES:

http://abcnews.com/sections/world/cia/kurdsnew.html

http://www.human rights.de/k/kurdistan

Index

Algiers Agreement, 17
Ataturk, Kemal, 21

Barzani, Mustafa, 19, **20**, 21
Berezendji, Mahmoud, 21
Byzantine Empire, the, 11

chador, **24**, 25
chemical weapons, 18
Christians, 11
Crusades, the, 11

France, 12, 14

Germany, 5
Great Britain, 12, 14, 20
Gulf War, the, 18

Halabja, 18, 26

Iran, 5, **10**, 14, 17-18, 19, 20-21,
    23, 26, 28
  and assistance to Kurds, 17
  and Islam, 21, 24, 25
Iran-Iraq War, 18, 21, 22
Iraq, 5, **10**, 11, 14, 16, 17-20, 21, 23, 28
  and chemical weapons, 18
  and Kurdish bombings, 19
Islam, 7, 11-12

Kurdish state, 12, 14, 21, 23, 28
Kurdistan, region of, 5, **10**, 15, 28
Kurdistan Workers Party, *see* PKK
Kurds
  and dress, 5, **8-9**, 21, **24**, 25, **27**
  and farming, 5-6, **22**, 23
  and illness, 18
  and language, 17, 21, 23, 25-26, 28
  nomadic lifestyle of, 5, 6-7
  origin of, 11

population of,
  in Germany, 5
  in Iraq, 20
  in Kurdistan region, 5, **10**
  worldwide, 26
  and religion, 7, 11-12
  and schooling, 17, 25-26
  and shepherding, 5-6

Medes, 11
Muslim, 7, 21, 24

oil, 21-22
Ottoman Empire, the, 7, 11-12

Persia, 7, 11, 20
peshmerga, 20
PKK, 22-23

refugees, 19, 21
resources, 21-22, 28

Saladin, 6, 12
sheikh, 7, 20-21
Sheikh Ubaidullah, 12, 20
Soviet Union, former, 14
Syria, 5, **10**, 12, 14, 23, 26

Treaty of Lausanne, 14, 17, 18
Treaty of Sèvres, 12, 15
Turkey, 5, **7**, **10**, 12, 18, 19, 21-23, 25, 28
  and PKK, 22-23

United States, 18

World War I, 12, 14
World War II, 21

Zahhak, 15
Zoroastrianism, 11

Items in bold print indicate illustration.